Arnold Kennedy

Merry Clappum Junction

The Strange Adventures of the New Zealand Express & a Boy

Arnold Kennedy

Merry Clappum Junction
The Strange Adventures of the New Zealand Express & a Boy

ISBN/EAN: 9783744678346

Printed in Europe, USA, Canada, Australia, Japan

Cover: Foto ©ninafisch / pixelio.de

More available books at **www.hansebooks.com**

Merry Clappum Junction

OR

THE STRANGE ADVENTURES

OF THE

New Zealand Express & A Boy

A QUICK TRAIN OF THOUGHT

WITH MUSIC

INTENDED FOR "CHILDREN OF ALL AGES"

BY

ARNOLD KENNEDY, M.A.

ASSOCIATE OF THE ROYAL ACADEMY OF MUSIC

LONDON

REMINGTON & CO.

1890

PREFACE.

AS regards the music in this book, the children's part will obviously be rather to listen than to perform in the first and last numbers, while the intermediate songs will be found well within their powers. It seems scarcely necessary to express obligation to the composers of two popular melodies, or to say that the rest of the music is by the writer of the story.

A contribution to Universal Folk-lore is offered in the chapter called "The House that Jack Built," and much light may (possibly) be shed by it upon the obscurities and omissions of an ancient nursery record.

Written at first merely to please the imagination of a few children, this little story is now given (or rather sold) to all who can resign themselves for a short time to a very simple kind of pleasure. Like the young persons who advertise their services as "companions," it professes to be nothing but "cheerful, musical, and domesticated."

Contents.

MERRY CLAPPUM JUNCTION.

CHAPTER I.

THE DEPARTURE.

IN a comfortable room of a house not far from Addition Road Station (Wax Candlington, W.), sat a small boy (with a long name) and a large dog (with a short name). The boy's name was Marmaduke, but his school-fellows, one and all, refused to call him by it. Some, who thought it too splendid, changed it to Marmalade, and others, who thought it too long, changed it to Tommy. The name of the dog was Winkle, which suited his character as a puppy much better than his present size and dignity. It was nearly dark in the street, and would have been quite dark in the room, but for the brilliant though uncertain light of a huge fire. In broad daylight the room had four corners, but just now it seemed to Tommy (as we shall call him) that it had a great many more: *how* many, he could not quite make out, for they "came out different," as he said to himself, every time he tried to count them. In this respect he thought they were extremely like sums in arithmetic, for Tommy was slow and backward at all lessons. He had often been told that what he heard in class went "in at one ear and out at the other," and he himself was inclined to think this a reasonable and natural explanation of his forgetfulness and other short-comings. That phrase came into his head, just as he had given up counting the corners of the room; and he applied it, oddly enough, to two musical perfor-mances which now began, one in the street and the other in an adjoining room. "If our own duet," he said to himself (his mother and sister were the performers), "goes in at my right ear and out of my left, then it will meet the street duet, which wants to come in at my left ear, and will keep it away; *our* duet will have gone through me, and so I shan't hear it any more, and the other duet will never get to me at all." In spite of this reasoning he continued to hear them both, but chiefly the trombone and flageolet outside, which were engaged upon "The Last Rose of Summer:" by an amicable arrangement, suited to the capacities of each instrument, the trombone went steadily through the melody, while the flageolet executed variations on its own account, the effect being something of this kind :—

THE LAST ROSE OF SUMMER.

The duets were not the only noises audible in the darkening room. " Other people's fathers," as Tommy expressed it, were walking home along the pavement, and their regular footfalls mingled with the bell of the muffin man, and were occasionally drowned altogether by the shriek of an engine whistle. The neighbouring station was an unalloyed pleasure to this boy, whatever it may have been to some of his elders. There was no detail connected with it, from shunting a goods train to clipping a ticket, which had not some interest for him; engine-drivers were his heroes of romance, and guards were beings at once delightfully and awfully* superior. He had often debated in his own mind whether he would be a guard or an engine-driver when he grew up ; that he could and would be one of the two, he did not doubt for a moment. As his thoughts now gradually wandered to that place of charm and mystery, the station, he said to himself, " I shall run round before tea and see the express come in from the city—the one that has new carriages and that only stops at Bewildering Junction and Fox-bridge Road. It's a little too early yet, though."

.   .   .   .

" Why, I am in the station !" he exclaimed. " I must have run very quick." It seemed strange that he could not remember putting on his cap and coming along the road, yet no doubt he had done so, for here was the familiar platform with a train ready to start. " I'm only just in time to see it," thought Tommy,

* The writer apologises to his young friends for using this word in an old-fashioned though not unnatural sense.

strolling along towards the engine. Two or three things presently struck him as odd, or at least as unexpected—for he had often before "met" the much respected express; one was the immense crowd of people on the platform, and the way in which they darted about incessantly in regular lines, as though they were playing some game, or trying to "describe" circles and triangles for the benefit of a Euclid class ; another was that no one seemed to be leaving the station as usual, but every one to be looking for a train to start by. It seemed strange, too, that there was a piano in the first-class waiting-room, which he had not noticed on his former visits. All his attention, however, was soon given to the bustle and talk all round him.

"Please label my box for Australia," said a young woman just behind him, "and don't forget to tie my photograph to the handle, then they'll know who I am." "By'r leave, lady," cried a porter dressed in green, who was carrying six or seven boxes on his head. "Oh, please," said another voice, "is this the

train for the Black Sea? I've been looking for it
since last Wednesday." "No, 'm; Black Sea train
doesn't start till next year; your Black Sea train
and your White Sea train run year and year about."
"What a lot of passengers there must be in those
trains!" said Tommy to the porter, who looked hard
at the boy, and then said in a low voice, " *There's never
any.*" Addition Road Station now seemed to Tommy
more wonderful than ever, and as he stood thinking
about the queer things he had heard, a tall guard
rang a bell close to his ear.

"Now, then, take your seats; get in,   get in,   get in,"...

sang the guard; "New Zealand Express! not stopping
this side of the North Pole," he shouted, adding in a
whisper to Tommy, "We don't stop this side of the
North Pole, and we don't stop on the other side either;
in fact we don't go that way at all. Now then, young
gentleman," he added in a louder voice, "where's your
ticket?" "I haven't got one," said Tommy ruefully,

" but I've got a new penknife and some toffey in
my pocket, and five shillings in a box at home."
The guard frowned. Then he wrote with a piece
of chalk on the side of the carriage, "The boy has
no ticket, but the boy has a penknife. The penknife
belongs to the boy. The boy has also toffey. Here
are five shillings. The shillings are in a box."

The passengers suddenly ceased running about, and
crowded round Tommy till he felt nearly smothered.
At that moment a tremendous whistle came from the
engine, and the train began to move. " They will all
be left behind," thought he; and no doubt they would
have been had not a troop of porters appeared and
thrown the people into the carriages. "Boys under
fifteen must fly; that's the rule," said the guard,
stamping wildly on the ground. Feeling quite certain
that he had to go by this train, like the other passengers, Tommy gave a little jump, and spread out his
arms as if he were in the water, and in a few moments
he was safely landed on the top of the carriage next
the engine. "They always told me that only birds

could fly," said he, much pleased with his own success. As the train steamed out of the station the guard jumped after the last carriage, and holding on for a moment with legs extended and coat-tails flying, he looked like an animated kite.

·"I don't want to go as far as New Zealand," thought Tommy, "I'll get out at the first station." He sat down, for curiously enough there was a chair on the top of the carriage; and then he noticed, much to his surprise, that Winkle was lying at his feet, asleep and apparently quite comfortable. After holding a short conversation (that was what he called it) with the dog, he was suddenly jerked about in an alarming manner, and he heard a clattering noise as though chimney-pots and tiles were falling on the pavement. He was not long in discovering the cause of all this, for, in fact, the train was running at great speed over the roofs of houses and leaping across the streets. There was really nothing to hold by, but Tommy put his hands on the dog's head, shut his eyes, pressed his lips together, and prepared for the worst.

CHAPTER II.

ISLE OF DOGS.

SPLASH, splash, splash! "I believe I've been asleep," said Tommy, as he looked up and saw that it was morning, and that the train was steaming down a river. The guard was standing over him and reading a geography book, from which he looked up occasionally to glance at the dog. "This dog ought to have a ticket," he said; "they all have them except the dog in the manger; *he* won't do anything regular." "Have you got a manger in this funny train?" asked Tommy. "We haven't got the manger," answered the guard, "but we've got the dog; I believe he is in my van at this moment. But you mustn't talk to the man

c

at the wheel, though he may talk to you." There *was* a wheel, as Tommy now saw, and the guard was steering the train by means of it, but his object seemed to be not to avoid the barges and steamers but to run into as many as possible. Every collision shook either the engine-driver or the stoker into the water ("they arrange to do that turn and turn about," the guard remarked), but there was no noise, and neither the train nor the vessels seemed any the worse.

Presently the river became more clear of shipping, and the guard began to give less attention to his wheel and more to his geography book. He glanced anxiously at the bank every now and then, as if he were looking out for some one. "It's about time the English master were here," he muttered. "Is that the English master?" asked Tommy presently, forgetting that he was not to speak, and pointing to a man in a long coat who was running along and keeping up with the train. The guard did not answer, but went on reading. The man on the bank was either playing a flute or pretending to play a ruler, as if it were a flute; it was hard to find out which, from the train. Suddenly he shouted to the guard, "Do you know the rule for finding New Zealand yet? You've had plenty of time to learn it." The guard stammered out, "You go by sea, and you go on, and on, and on till YOU SEE LAND." He whispered to Tommy, "This one likes puns—such good ones as *I* make;" but if the English master was pleased, he certainly did not show it, for he only called out, "I expect you'd remember the rule better if you had the ruler," and immediately something hard whizzed close to the guard's head and fell into the water. "He's not going to ask *me* any questions," thought Tommy with a sigh of relief, for the man had seated himself on the bank and was apparently going to sleep.

A few minutes later the train sidled up to the bank and stopped. "Isle of Dogs," cried the guard, "all dogs change here!" Tommy did not think there were any dogs in the train except his own, but in this he was wrong. Dogs of every kind he had ever seen jumped and scrambled out of the carriage windows without waiting to have the doors opened or stopping to give up their tickets. "Were they dogs when they got in?" he asked. "Yes, to be sure," answered the guard, "every paw of them. Some were funny dogs, some were sly dogs, some were sad dogs, and some lead a cat-and-dog life." This explanation did not really make the subject clear to the boy, but it took off his attention from Winkle, who had followed the other dogs, and was now slowly and deliberately trotting away. Before Winkle's master noticed this proceeding, or remembered that he had intended to get out himself at the first station, the train was steaming away from the bank. Determined not to be carried off, Tommy jumped—unfortunately, into the water.

CHAPTER III.

CLAPPUM JUNCTION.

OMMY quite believed that he could swim to land, but he certainly did not expect that the land would come to him. Yet this was just what happened; after he had made a few strokes the water gradually sank away, and at last he found himself moving his legs and arms about on soft dry grass. When he had done this for a few minutes, it occurred to him that there was a simpler way of getting along than that, and he got up to walk away. It was well he did so, for just as he turned to find out what had become of the river, he saw the train making for

him at a high speed, and he would certainly have
been run over had not the engine suddenly lowered
its funnel, caught him up and thrown him back to
his old place on the top of the carriage. "We've
been looking for you for hours," said the guard. "I
thought it was only a few minutes," said Tommy;
"where is that river gone to?" "Flowed away," said
the guard; "rivers never stand still."

Tommy was very much relieved to find that the
train was now running smoothly along rails in the
manner of trains in general. He was surprised to
notice that it was now getting dark, and he tried in
vain to think why this day and the previous night
had passed away so quickly, "with almost nothing in
them," as he expressed it. It was all the darker,
because the train was running through a wood, behind which the setting sun was just visible. Oddly
enough, the wood was quite as thick in front of the
train as it was on each side; and just as Tommy
thought there would be a collision with the trees in

front, they opened out and then closed again behind the train. "There's not much to see," he thought, but it was a fine thing not to be told to go to bed, and he determined to keep awake as long as he could; indeed he was a little afraid of falling off the carriage.

The guard seemed to be half asleep already. The driver and stoker had made up a sort of bed on the tender, and on this they lay down, after fastening a printed notice to the side of the engine: COWS ARE EARNESTLY REQUESTED NOT TO UPSET THE TRAIN. Tommy hoped very much that this would prove a safe way of travelling, but it needed all his customary respect for engine-drivers to keep him from suspecting that there was something wrong about these proceedings. However, his thoughts soon wandered to other things, and just as he was wondering how many, if any of the original passengers were still in the train, the sound of a flageolet came up from a window of the carriage on which he was sitting, and

after a few notes of accompaniment some one began
to sing. The singer and the player were at opposite
windows, and both seemed to be trying how far they
could lean out without actually falling on to the
line.

THE TRAVELLER'S SONG.

1. Oh! large is the world and
2. Now, if you are sad and

round as   a ball, But look where you will, You'll find no place at all   Like
do not know why, Come, pluck up your cour-age and tra - vel with I   To

Quasi recit.

After verses 1-7. |D.C.| After verse 8.

Merry Clappum Junction.

f a tempo.   D.C.   *mf*   *pp*

3. Or if you are pining for something to do,
   Go, learn off by heart all the trains that run through
       Or stop at Clappum Junction.

4. Some love the high mountains, some love the wide sea,
   Some love the green lanes of the country, but we
       Delight in Clappum Junction.

5. There is not a delicate * under the sun
   So dear as a sandwich, so sweet as a bun,
       Procured at Clappum Junction.

6. It's good for a headache, it's good for a cold,
   It's good for the young and it's good for the old
       To stop at Clappum Junction.

7. You may start from Quebec, you may start from Japan;
   You may start from Herne Bay, yet you (probably) can
       Book through to Clappum Junction.

7. You may start from Que - bec, you may start from Ja - pan, You may

8. Then don't lose your temper, and don't lose your way;
   Let nothing whatever induce you to say,
       "Oh, bother Clappum Junction!"

---

* "Sir, you have fed us with delicates."—*Old Book on Etiquette.*

D

Tommy had interrupted the song after the sixth verse by leaning over the carriage to ask the singer, " *Why* is it good for a headache ? " " If you stop there with a headache," he answered, " of course your head stops aching; that's as plain as a signal-box."

The refrain of each verse had been taken up in chorus by the other passengers. It was nearly dark when the song was finished, and as the last voice sang, or rather shouted, " Clappum Junction," Tommy saw a number of lights twinkling some distance in front of the train. As the lights grew larger, he made out the platforms of a station, crowded with people who were holding out their arms like signals; but though they shouted and stamped, they failed to awaken the driver or the stoker, and the train rushed through Clappum Junction at full speed. Then the trees moved together and closed in behind the train, and the station was quite hidden from view.

CHAPTER IV.

HALF AN HOUR FOR BREAKFAST.

THE train now stopped of itself, but the men on the engine slept calmly on. The guard, however, awoke, and seizing Tommy by the arm exclaimed, "Boy! where is Clappum?" "I couldn't help it," said Tom ; "the engine-driver and the stoker were both asleep, and we ran right through the station." "The varlets!" cried the guard ; "clap 'em in irons!" With that he drew from his pockets, to the boy's astonishment, a poker and shovel, and giving them to Tommy told him to tie the men to the nearest tree. "What with?" asked Tommy. "With these irons, of course," said the guard. "I know I can't do that," said Tommy; "it's impossible!" "You can do anything if you try," said the guard, "and besides, I'm going to help you, and *I* can do anything even if I don't try." Encouraged by this remark, but feeling still a little doubtful, Tommy helped the guard to roll the men on to the grass, and managed without waking them to tie them fast to a tree, the poker and shovel suddenly becoming as soft as ropes in his hands. He began to think he must be dreaming, but soon changed his mind when he found (1) that his eyes were open, and (2) that there was a squirrel looking down upon him from a large beech tree. "If I were asleep," he said, "my eyes would be shut, and a squirrel couldn't climb on anything but a real tree."

The guard stood close by and looked at the sleeping men with his head a little on one side. "That's most furious and fast," he said; "they couldn't get loose even if they was ever so good." "They couldn't get loose," said the squirrel, "even if nuts was apples."

"That's bad grammar," said Tommy decidedly; he had wanted to correct the guard, but he didn't like to. "Grammar," said the squirrel, "what's that?" "Oh, grammar," said Tommy. "Why, of course, grammar's what you say—I mean what you do—no, what you say when you—when——" but at this moment the guard began to ring his bell, and Tommy was not very sorry that he couldn't finish his sentence. "First bell," shouted the guard; "get out of bed, you boys." "I *am* out of bed," said Tommy indignantly. "I've not been in bed all night." (He couldn't remember when it got light, but it was certainly now a clear sunny morning.) "So much the *bedder*," said the guard, and he rang the bell again; this time he shouted, "Breakfast bell, breakfast bell!"

Tommy saw now that the train was quite full of passengers, and he wondered in a confused way whether they were the passengers who had started with the train, or whether those had all been mysteriously changed into dogs before they reached the

river.   Whoever they were, they got very impatient
at the long delay, and tried in vain to open the doors.
Some held out their umbrellas and hit the side of
the carriage ("just like people do to omnibus con-
ductors," Tommy remarked, and happily neither the
guard nor the squirrel said anything about *his* grammar); others waved their pocket-handkerchiefs, and all
seemed to be talking at the top of their voices.   But
instead of unlocking the doors the guard merely said,
"There really isn't breakfast enough for such a crowd,
but I'll sing them a song to comfort them."   So the
guard sang this song:—

THE BREAKFAST SONG.

1. E - nough for one, e-nough for two, but not e-nough for

all our crew, But not e-nough for all our crew.

D.S. Last verse ends.

2. Then if you can.

col. 8.

2. Then weigh your anchor, sail away
   Until you come to Biscay's bay.

3. And when the waves roll long and high,
   For breakfast you will never sigh ;

4. Or if to breakfast down you sit,
   You will not eat one little bit.

5. But when you see the coast of Spain
   Your appetite will come again.

6. And when we reach the flowing Nile
   Perhaps we'll meet a crocodile.

7. If we a crocodile should see,
   I think we'd run away from *he.*

8. Then comes Australia (I speak true),
   And there we'll see a kangaroo.

9. I'll leave you there (that is my plan)
   To find New Zealand if you can.

"I suppose it'll send them to sleep," Tommy thought, as the song was proceeding; "people seem to be always falling asleep on this journey;" and he was right, for at the end of the song all the passengers were quiet, sleeping as they had stood when awake, with umbrellas held stiff, and handkerchiefs waving gently in the breeze. Tommy laughed, and the guard said triumphantly, "There! your common barn-door musician couldn't have managed that! People always do that when *I* sing." "But I don't see any breakfast laid," said Tommy, speaking rather wistfully. "To tell the truth," said the guard, "there isn't any; but still there would be less for us if all those people were here, that's quite plain." "I don't understand that," said Tommy sadly. "I daresay not," said the guard. "You can't expect to understand things if you didn't arrange about it at the booking-office before you started. But cheer up. If the worst comes to the worst, we—— But what is become of those bold bad men whom you fastened to the tree?"

The guard had turned round and discovered that the engine-driver and stoker had disappeared. Then he added more gently, "One was bold and the other was bad, and they have both faded away, like summer's last rose." Tommy scarcely noticed the guard's words, for he was watching the poker and shovel walking away through a narrow path among the trees. "You see," said the guard, "they have tied themselves together at the top in order that they may have two legs between them." "I wonder what has become of the men," thought Tommy. "Why, of course they've gone back to their *post*," said the guard; "if we had tied them to one they'd have been quite happy." It always took Tommy some time to understand the guard's puns, and while he was thinking about this one he heard the engine begin to snort. In a few moments the train was making off, and as it disappeared he saw the stoker sitting astride the engine, waving a lump of coal in the air, and he heard the passengers give one great shout of triumph.

E

CHAPTER V.

THE COUNCIL OF BEASTS.

WHEN the guard saw that there was no chance of catching the train, he said to Tommy and the squirrel, "Before I show you how very sorry I am for this unfortunate occurrence, I must sing a song about it. I always set my troubles to music. Then he began to look extremely cheerful, and sang:—

[*Music is on page* 36.]

When the song was ended, the guard groaned and wrung his hands; "That's enough happiness for the present," he said. The squirrel had been trying hard to beat time to the song; but by the end of the first verse it began to look puzzled, and at the last verse it gave it up with a sigh. "It would be more sensible," it remarked, "if you would ring your bell instead of your hands. If you can't find the way to New Zealand, you must advertise it, and offer a reward. Some of the beasts or birds or fishes in the wood are sure to have heard something of it. Even *I* might give you some information if you asked me very nicely."

The guard then rang a loud peal, and shouted, "Lost, at or about this present time, the way to New Zealand! Whoever will discover it, and bring it to my address, will be REWARDED. Whoever does not discover it will be PUNISHED. If they don't come to get the reward," he remarked, "they are sure to come to get off being punished." A great rustling and tramping was now heard, as an army of animals of every kind trooped up from all directions, while birds arranged themselves in rows on every branch of the nearest trees. A kangaroo, a canary, a cat, a crocodile, a camel and a cuttle-fish came to the front and

CONSOLATION SONG.*

Con dolore.

1. Oh
2. Oh

p   *legato*

where and oh where has my mer - ry train disap-peared to? It has gone to bright New
why and oh why has it started be - fore its time? You must ask the sta - tion-

Zea - land, if it can find the way; But it's my decided op - inion that it might
mast - er, that's what I say to you; Then shout for points and sleepers and the

* To judge by the absence of rhyme and the uncertain number of syllables, the words of this song must have been made up by the guard as he went along. It is hoped that the *bars* marked in verse 3 will show sufficiently how it is to be sung. The last verse seems to require more explicit treatment.

just as well have stayed where it was!
sig - nal - man so free! 4. For it's gay and bold and free, that is to say

life on a rail - way train. Then ho! , for the sleep - ers, and

hi! for the points and

3. Oh | when, and oh | when shall we | see its face once | more?
You must | look it up in | Bradshaw and | the-e-en you'll | know;
So-o | shout for points and sleepers, and the | signalman so free!

seemed inclined to speak. "You see they all begin
with a K," said the squirrel, nodding pleasantly to
Tommy, who was beginning to say "They don't," when
the crocodile called out "Silence!" in such a terrible
voice that the camel shivered, and the hairs of the cat
stood up on end. Then the crocodile said, "I want to
know why breakfast isn't ready, and I'll thank some
one to tell me pretty quick. As soon as this business
is over, I must be off to Egypt, and I'll thank some
one to find me a train to go by." Then he smiled.
The guard looked nervous. "There are some very
nice sandwiches at Clappum Junction," he said in a
low voice, "real old Egyptians, very dry. But first,
I wish this meeting would tell us the way to New
Zealand." "Oh, that's easy enough," said all the
creatures at once. Then the cuttle-fish spread out its
feelers, and said with a yawn, "You go by sea, you
know: any fish could tell you that. We're always
going there." "How long does it take?" said Tommy
timidly. "I can't tell you that," said the cuttle-fish,

"because I never managed to get there." "You take a fly," said the canary, "that's the easiest way, and the cheapest too." The kangaroo said, "You should go to Australia and then ask again." Here the camel was seized with a violent fit of laughter: he was understood to begin "In the *long run*," and then he nearly choked. The crocodile looked at the camel very severely and said, "If you think you are the only person who can *joke*, you're much mistaken." When the camel had quite recovered itself, the cat said that she didn't see why they should go to New Zealand at all, as the train would get on quite well without them. For that matter, she didn't see why anybody should trouble to go so far. Then the crocodile shrieked out, "If you don't settle this business before the earth turns round another inch, I shall eat you up, every one of you, and then get some Clappiam sandwiches for dessert." At this the squirrel chimed in: "Did I understand you to say that the earth was turning round?" "I don't know whether you understood me," growled the crocodile, "but that's what I said, neither fewer nor manyer." "*I* know," said Tommy eagerly; "the earth turns round on its axis once every twenty-four hours." "I don't see the use of having axes to turn round upon," said the squirrel; "but if the earth turns round so quickly as that, you have only to get up in the air, and New Zealand will come round to you." . . . . .

CHAPTER VI.

ACROSS ENGLAND IN THE AIR.

"WHERE are we?" said Tommy, "and where have the beasts gone to?" After thinking a little he came to the conclusion that he was really trying the squirrel's new plan for taking long journeys. His next thought was that the guard might just as well have gone alone, as he himself had no wish to go to New Zealand without telling his friends at home. Still here he was, balancing himself in the air, while trees, rivers, and towns rushed past him with a noise like the wind. Not far off was the guard, holding a map in one hand and a sandwich in the other; he seemed to find the sandwich very tough, and the map very puzzling. "It won't do to miss anything, now we've started," he said. But Tommy only answered, "I'm very hungry, and I don't want to go to New Zealand at all, but I wish I could find my dog." "As to hunger," said the guard, "that all depends on how you take it. I thought I was hungry till I took *this*" (shaking the sandwich about impatiently); "now I don't think I am. I should like to drop it, only I am afraid it will hurt some one."

As the country rushed past underneath them, the guard began to look very disappointed. "It's not a bit like the map," he said; "all the counties seem to be the same colour, and they've got no shape at all." Suddenly Tommy looked down to a field that was flying away from them, and saw his dog trotting gently along and just about to get over a stile. "I *won't* go any further," he shouted, "I'll just shake myself down." So he shook himself down, and when he found that this was quite easy to do he wondered why he had not done it before. "I believe you can do anything in this country when once you think of it," he said to himself as he proceeded to follow his dog.

He felt just a little sorry to part with the guard, who seemed to be flying off rapidly, and who gave him a friendly nod as he disappeared. "Remember, double breakfast to-morrow, to make up: no crocodiles admitted!" said the guard, and in a minute or two he was lost in the distance.

CHAPTER VII.

THE HOUSE THAT JACK BUILT.

TOMMY ran on, panting and whistling to his dog. Winkle took no notice of these attentions, and crossed one stile after another, keeping always one field ahead of his pursuer. As Tommy was beginning to think he had crossed all the stiles in the world, he saw a large bare wall not far ahead extending an immense way to the right and left, and so high that he could not see the top of it. "Winkle can't get over that," thought he, but when he reached the wall no Winkle was to be seen.

A little girl with a violin in her hand stood knocking at a small door; it seemed the only door in the whole wall, and there were no windows. When the door opened Tommy followed the girl into a low passage. She was waving her violin about, and the air seemed to be playing upon it. "That's what you call an *air*," she said. "I wish I could play my scales like that," said Tommy. The girl turned round and said, "Talking about scales, did you happen to see a crocodile before you came in?" "There was one at our meeting," said Tommy; "we had a meeting of beasts, you know." "I daresay it was the same," said the little girl. "He was eating a sandwich when I met him, and he said it had dropped from the clouds. Then he asked me whether sandwiches often dropped from the clouds in England; because if they did, he thought he would stay here. He looked rather cross when I told him that I had never seen any come that way, and I was afraid he would eat me, but he said he had a kind heart under his scales. He also asked me the way to a place called Clappiam Jungle, where sandwiches grew, but I told him that I had never heard of it. Just then a train ran past (they don't often come round this way, because they have to get over the stiles), and the crocodile ran after it."

"I wish you would tell me," said Tommy, "where my dog went; I saw him a few minutes ago." "You can't expect to keep on seeing things," said the girl, "and I don't know anything about *your* dog; you may take ours if you like." "Then can you tell me who *you* are," said Tommy, "and what this house is called?" "I can do that quite easily," said the girl, as she put her fiddle away in a cupboard. "This is the house that Jack built, and I am Miss Jack. There's a story about us which you may have read. They sing it sometimes; in fact, they generally sing it when any one listens." After saying this the girl sat down and seemed to be going to sleep; she just said in a drowsy voice, "One has to listen, and the other has to go to sleep." Tommy listened, and though he did not discover who "they" were, he heard a note struck on a piano, and then some voices began to sing very softly:

THE HOUSE THAT JACK BUILT.

This is the house that Jack built. This is the malt that lay in the house that Jack built. This is the rat that ate the malt that lay in the house that Jack built.

This is the cat that killed the rat that ate the malt that lay in the house that

Jack built — This is the dog that

wor-ried the cat that killed the rat that ate the malt that lay in the house that

Jack built.
This is the cow with the crumpled
accelerando e cres.
a tempo.
cres.
horn that tossed the dog that wor-ried the cat that killed the rat that
ate the malt that lay in the house that Jack built.
p This is the
p

mf
maid - en all for - lorn that milked the cow with the crum-pled horn that
Allegro.
dim.
tossed the dog that wor-ried the cat that killed the rat that ate the malt that
poco rall.
Andante (MM. ♩. = 60.)
MM. ♩. = 70.
lay in the house that Jack built.
This is the

man all tat-tered and torn, that kiss-ed the maid-en all forlorn, that milked the

cow with the crumpled horn, that tossed the dog that worried the cat that

killed the rat that ate the malt that lay in the house that Jack built.

This is the priest all sha-ven and shorn that married the

man all tat-tered and torn that kissed the mai - den all for - lorn that milked the

cow with the crumpled horn That tossed the dog that worried the cat that killed the rat that ate the malt, that lay in the house that Jack built.

This is the cock that crowed in the morn, That

waked the priest all shav-en and shorn, That married the man all tattered and torn, That kissed the maid - en, all   for - lorn, That milked the cow with the crum-pled horn,   That

Presto.   *rall.*

tossed the dog   that wor-ried the cat, That killed the rat that ate   the malt, That

Andante.

lay in the house that Jack   built.

mf

f

mf

Ped.

When the music came to an end Miss Jack woke up and said, "The malt is gone, of course, because the rat ate it, and father hadn't the heart to get any more. It was a great disappointment to him; he said he would never trust rats any more." Tommy looked puzzled and Miss Jack added, "He was our own pet rat, and he assured us that he was quite honest; he said that he wished to be in the malt-cellar in order to kill the mice that tried to eat the malt. When we reproached him afterwards, he said the mice had eaten the malt, and he had eaten the mice. I didn't want father to punish him, but the cat came and killed him before I could say anything." "What does Mr. Jack do now?" said Tommy. "You'll see presently," said the little girl; "he is the last thing in the house."

Miss Jack now led the way through a long straight passage, from which doors opened on each side. All the rooms that they passed were furnished alike, and Tommy remarked to Miss Jack that he wouldn't

know one from another. "Neither do we," she
answered; "that's the fun of it. There is one for
every day of the year, and they are all on the ground-
floor." "Did you punish the cat?" asked Tommy.
"Oh no, poor thing!" said Miss Jack. "We couldn't
punish everybody—the cat and the cow and the cock
and the tattered man; so we gave all the punishments
to the dog. He is kept tied up, and is always fed on
sprats." "I think you're very unkind," said Tommy;
"it was the cat's fault just as much. What's the dog's
name?" "We took away his name when we tied him
up," said Miss Jack. "He has such a temper that
he'd worry his own name if he had one."

Talking in this way, the boy and girl walked on
through the passage. Tommy was getting hungry,
and he noticed that it had gradually become very hot.
"We're more than half through the year now," said
Miss Jack; "this part is called *Allroast*; it will be
cooler when we reach *Allover*, and at *Stovember* we
shall want fires." "What a quick sort of year!" said

Tommy. "What do you do when you've got to the end of it?" "We just begin again," answered Miss Jack. She paused a little, and then continued: "I suppose you're going to ask about the cow with the crumpled horn now? I'll tell you, at all events. The cow is in the shed, and the crumpled horn is in the twenty-seventh music-cupboard." "I don't think I understand," said Tommy. "It's a French horn," said Miss Jack; "father plays on it when there's company. It was the cow that crumpled it by tossing it about. When she got tired of tossing the horn, she tossed the dog. She also tossed the man who came to write the story about us, but he didn't say anything about that." "And the maiden all forlorn?" "She married the gatekeeper, you know," said Miss Jack. "He has new clothes now, and lives in the lodge behind the house. He hasn't much to do, because people always come in at the front door." "Do people go out by the lodge?" asked Tommy; "your front wall looked so high and long that I don't see how I'm to get home,

unless I go back through this passage." "Nobody
goes back that way," said Miss Jack positively;
"when *we* get to the end of the year the front of the
house comes round to the other side, but the people
who come to see us disappear when they reach the
backyard. *I* don't know what becomes of them; I
expect they go to nothing."

Tommy became a little alarmed; he did not want
to "go to nothing" at all—indeed he felt a little
inclined to cry. Miss Jack continued: "The priest
has just given us a week's notice; he says he can't
sleep because of that noisy cock." They had now got
past the 300th room, as Tommy saw by the numbers
on the doors. In the 350th room a nice breakfast
was laid. "I wish we could go in and have some,"
said Tommy, stopping short: "I see some sausage-
rolls." "That's not to-day's breakfast," said Miss
Jack; "if you tried to eat that, the things wouldn't
come away from the plates. But come along and see
father making his fiddle."

In a room marked 365 a man was sitting on a
table cross-legged. In one hand he had a pocket-
knife, and in the other some string; on his lap lay a
large block of wood. The words, "Jack, violin-maker
to Her Majesty," were written upon the wall. A
violin lay near him, apparently as a model, at which
he occasionally glanced. He tied the string round
the wood, and then took it off and tied it round the
knife; then he laid the knife on the wood, and tied
the string round both of them. As the boy and girl
came in, he looked up with a puzzled face but said
nothing. "Do you make violins?" asked Tommy.
"I haven't made one yet," answered Mr. Jack, "but
I'm busy making one; it will be so different from
other violins that you can play in all keys at once,
and one tune will sound exactly like another. That's
what you call success." Tommy didn't know what to
say to this, so he only asked if he might see the dog
and have some breakfast. "As to breakfast," said
Mr. Jack, "if you can manage to keep from disappear-

ing while the house turns round, you can have New
Year's Day's breakfast with us; and as to the dog——"
Mr. Jack stopped, jumped on to the floor, and felt
Tommy's pulse." "I expect you're pretty brave," he
said, "because your hair is so curly; but the dog
is *most* ferocious." "Does he bite people?" asked
Tommy. "He hasn't bitten anybody *yet*," said Mr.
Jack, "but he would if he were not tied up. Even
the postman is afraid of him, though *he* never comes
nearer than the front door."

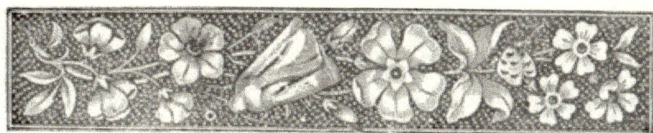

CHAPTER VIII.

A MYSTERIOUS DISAPPEARANCE.

TOMMY followed Mr. and Miss Jack into a yard behind the house. A man in very new clothes was standing by the door of a cottage; hanging round his neck was a card, on which were printed the words, "Once I was tattered and torn!" His wife was leaning out of the cottage window playing a concertina. Another man, with a portmanteau in his hand, was opening a little gate to go out. "That must be the priest," thought Tommy, "and there *is* a way out after all." A cock just then craned his neck towards the priest, and uttered one deafening crow. The cat was sitting on a stumpy apple-tree licking her lips; the cow was lowing gently in an out-house. As to the

dog, he was tied to a kennel by six chains attached
to different parts of his body—one to each leg, one to
his tail, and one to his neck; and he was half covered
up by printed bills, telling people to "Beware of the
dog." He seemed to be lying very quiet, however, and
certainly had not taken the trouble to worry the bills.

All at once everything became so still that Tommy
began to think he was looking at a picture. The
priest was standing motionless at the open gate; the
woman was holding her concertina without playing on
it; the cow had ceased lowing. Just then he heard
Miss Jack say, "Now he's going to disappear." He
tried to turn round, but he found he could not move.
Miss Jack went on talking, but her voice sounded
fainter and fainter, and she seemed to be moving
away. "He wants to know if we're a picture: he
wants to know if *he's* a picture: he wants to—know—
if——" Then there was a sound as of some huge
weight being pushed along the ground. "If Miss
Jack is moving round with the house," thought

Tommy, "she'll be still at the back, and the front will come round to me. Then I'll cross the stiles again, and go home by Clappum Junction and the river. At any rate, I won't disappear."

No; he was not disappearing at all, but the things and people in the yard seemed to be "changing about" in a very strange way. Was that a cock or a crocodile? The cow-shed seemed half a shed and half an engine. He could not make out what instrument the woman had in her hand; every time he looked it was something different. He tried once more to move, and this time he succeeded. There was a chair behind him, and feeling suddenly drowsy, he sat down. "I believe it's getting dark again," he thought; "what a long time I've been away! I wish I could go home." Then he shut his eyes, but he found that they would not "come open" again. The priest went out at last, banging the door after him; but immediately after, some one opened the door and seemed to come up to the dog and move the bills about with a rustling noise. The woman played a loud chord on what sounded like a piano, and then Tommy heard what he afterwards described as a "great mixed noise:" it was made up, he said, of falling tiles, rushing water, the whistle of an engine, the voice of a crocodile, and the shouting of porters. Then all was silent. With a great effort he opened his eyes, and saw his father turning over a newspaper, his mother rising from the piano in the next room, and his sister putting a violin away. Before he quite realised where he was, a gentle voice said, "Why are you looking so frightened, Tommy?" Tommy only answered, "I was frightened because Miss Jack said I was going to disappear. And you're a jolly old Wink, and I wonder how you got over that wall"—this was said to the dog, of course—"and, mother, may I have some supper?"

PRINTED BY BALLANTYNE, HANSON AND CO., EDINBURGH AND LONDON.